REST IS BEST

For the Workaholic in your Life

Shakti A. Burke

Text and illustrations © 2019 Shakti A. Burke

All rights reserved. No part of this book may be reproduced or transmitted in any form or by any means, without the express written permission of the publisher. A person who does an unauthorised act in relation to this publication may be liable to criminal prosecution and civil claims for damages.

First edition 2019

ISBN 978-0-6484796-0-4

Published by Joyful Mind
Black Horse Creek
Kyogle NSW Australia

www.joyfulmind.net.au

follow joyfulmind on instagram and facebook

If you enjoy this book, please leave an online review!

dedicated to
my four fabulous sisters
Mary, Margaret, Jane and Julia

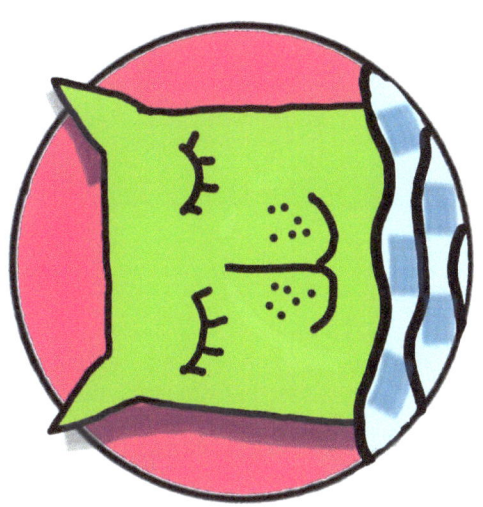

joyfulmind.net.au

Modern life is such
that we
drive ourselves on
mercilessly.

Grind on forward,
stop at nil,
push that boulder
up the hill.

Work long hours,
never home,
neglect our spiritual
chromosome.

Fight our way
unto the top,
pump and pressure
never stop.

But think about it:
is it wise
to bring about
our own demise?

To reach the zesty
crest of best
we really need to
slot in rest.

Human body
was not made
for unrelenting
escapade.

Human brain
was never meant
for unremitting
punishment.

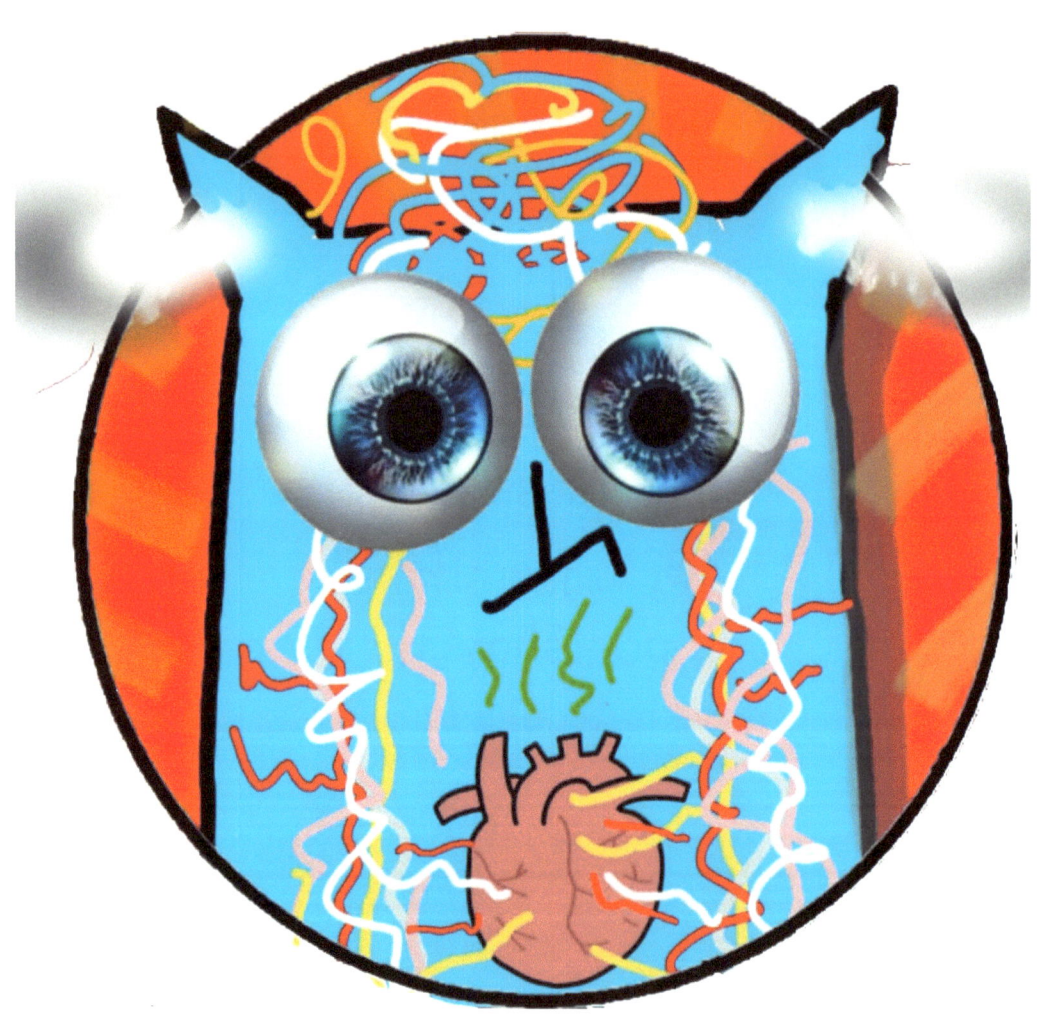

Nervous system
not designed for
constant wear and tear
combined.

And if you think
work-till-you-drop
is the best way
to get on top ...

then Sir or Madam
I suggest
to treat yourself
and think of rest.

A rest can be a song,
a dance, a laugh,
a chat, a take the chance
to walk, to swim, to take the time.
How'd chillin'-out
become a crime?

Take a break from
push and shove,
devote time
to the things you love.

Rest doesn't have
a money cost,
it gives you back
the spark
you've lost.

It gives you back
your very self:
now ain't that just
the best of wealth?

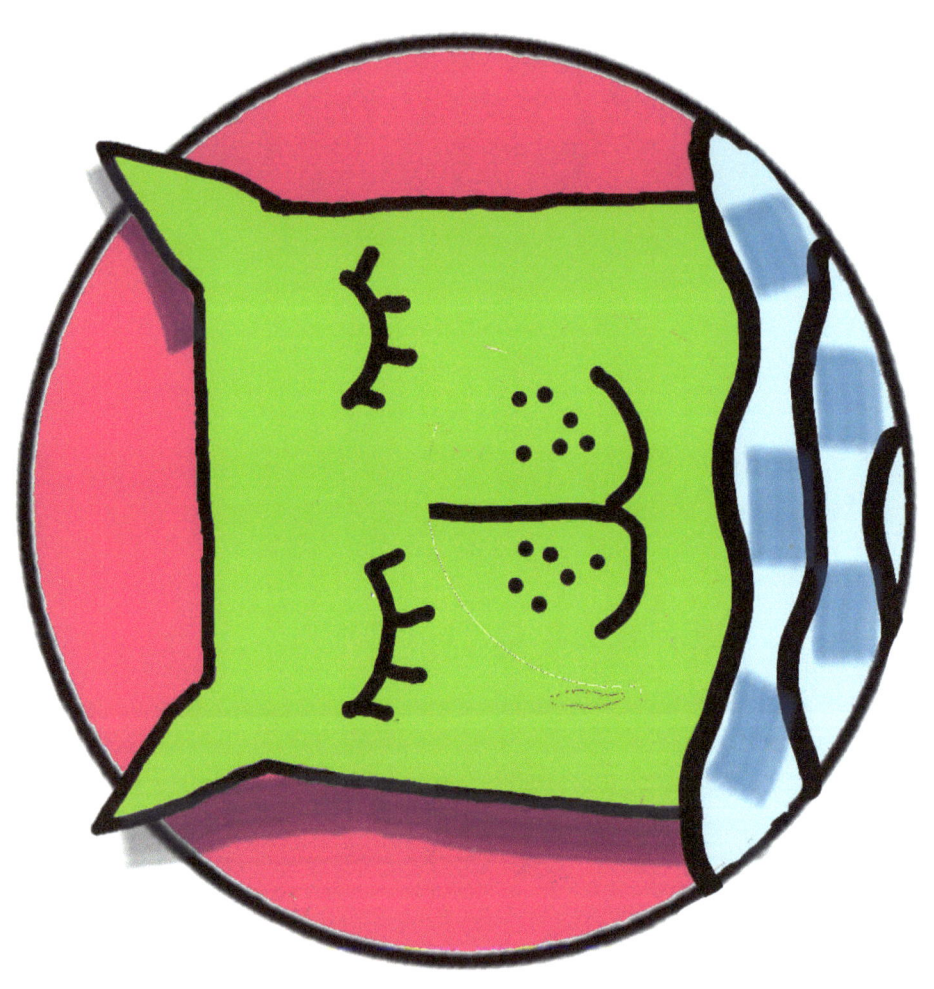

A rest can simply be a kip,
a short, a sweet refreshing dip.
A power nap, a micro rest
will have you firing
at your best.

It's best kept short
10 mins or 20
for replenishment
a-plenty.

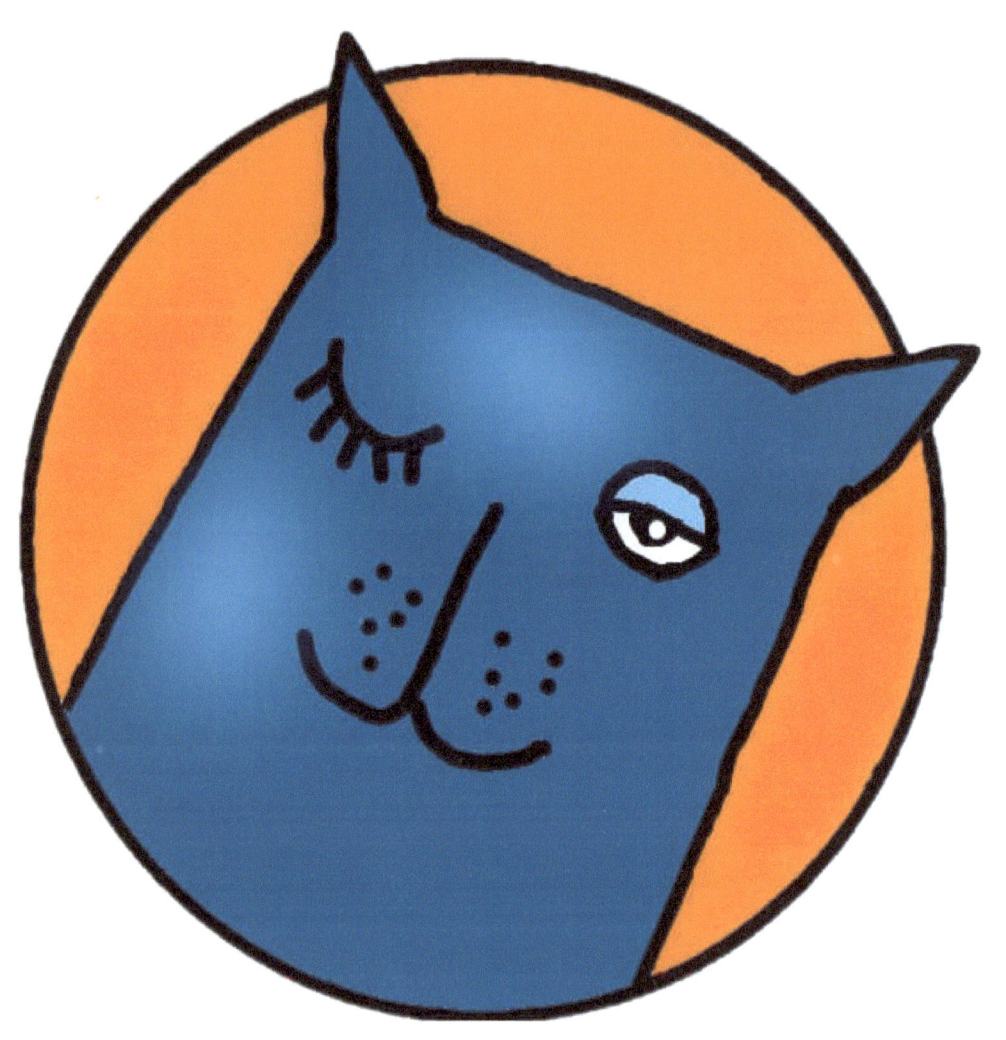

Steer away from
hours-long snooze,
with groggy feeling
hard to lose.

Wouldn't it be great
if we could make
our workplace thrive,
by calling on the power of rest
to reboot and revive?

Studies show that
we should all be
working less, not more.
Tell your boss that burnout
burns out profit,
that's for sure.

Stress costs the economy
billions every year.
Rest tops up brain glucose
and kicks brain cells
into gear.

Raise the banner, gild the crest,
spell out every letter:
resting is not idleness and
busy is not better.

Resting is the secret sauce,
the golden snitch, the key resource,
the silver bullet, tiger's eye,
a principle to live life by.

Supporter, ally,
best-est friend.
The benefits of rest
don't end.

Just a tip:
at rest's conclusion,
when you're done with
quiet seclusion,
pause before you up-and-go,
to bask in rest's warm afterglow:

... a special nurturing
inner space.
Don't barge straight
past this lovely place!

When I rest I feel
more whole,
I feel at peace within
my soul.

When I rest I feel more bright,
more balanced, buoyed
and smart
and light.

When I rest I feel more like
I'm up on top,
I'm near the spike.
I've reached the place I want to be,
because I've come back home to me.

So all that striving, force and will,
and all that
pushing up the hill,
itself can find relief and rest.
And that's the part
I like the best.

REASONS TO
R.E.S.T.

R   Rest. Relax. Renew. Recharge. Recuperate. Restoration. Resilience. Regeneration

E   Everything Else becomes more Effortless..Effective. Efficient. It's Empowering, Enriching, Enabling.

S   Science supports the power and effectiveness of Rest. Studies show a nap of about 20 minutes in the afternoon has a positive effect on attention, vigilance, mood and alertness. Napping increases creativity and task performance, raises stamina, lifts mood, improves problem-solving and renews cognitive function.

T   Take the time to rest: it's worth it!
Discover for yourself what suits you best.
It could be a "yoga nidra" relaxation.
Or a powernap for 15 minutes to a voice track, music or an audiobook. Or in front of the tv.
Timer: use a timer to prevent over-snoozing leading to a sleep hangover.

Time is our most precious resource.
Resting creates more time in the day, due
to the efficiency of a refreshed brain.
By managing our daily energy quotas better
through regular rest, we get more done, in less
time, with reduced wear and tear.

RESOURCES

YOGA NIDRA POWER NAP

find guided audios on:
You Tube, Soundcloud, Spotify, iTunes
and Insight Timer

Recommended
Morven Hamilton (UK)
Mar Healy (Ireland
Shakti Burke (Australia)
Manoj Dias (Australia)

laurentober.com/blog
My mindfulness blog: www.joyfulmind.net.au/blog

LINKS

www.theenergyproject.com
www.napnow.net.au
www.irest.org
www.tinybuddha.com
www.zenhabits.net
www.joyfulmind.net.au

Picture credits via Shutterstock and PNG Tree:
blue67design, Diego Schtutman, ezzat

sarvam mangalam

www.ingramcontent.com/pod-product-compliance
Lightning Source LLC
Chambersburg PA
CBHW042348300426
44110CB00032B/63